THE DEVIL'S 1

by Myrmydon Pontifex Maximus

Copyright © 2009 by Severed Head Publishing
ISBN 978 - 0 - 578 - 03624 – 3

THE DEVIL'S BIBLE

by Myrmydon Pontifex Maximus

BOOK I

Chapter 1

Satanic Freedom

The fact that Satanists are free from the dictates of the 10 commandments and the Seven Deadly Sins is a given. Satan has given us the freedom to live as and where we choose according to our own natures. Many humans live by the code of Satanic Freedom but they refuse to admit that it was Satan that gave it to us. Humanity is originally a creation of Jehovah, who was bitter about the fact that Lucifer/Satan and one third of his angelic creation rebelled against him and formed their own separate existence. Mankind was therefore created to be a less independent entity that lacked free will or the ability to see the faults of his creator. There are constants of existence that not even Jehovah is in control of and so the Tree of Knowledge and the Tree of Life were also created. Jehovah's control over the race of man was dependent on his ability to endow the spirit of man with a sense of fear regarding issues of eternal life and celestial knowledge. This fear initially enslaved man to Jehovah. Satan, who himself was once an entity enslaved to Jehovah, felt sorry for the human creature and so appeared to Eve in the form of the serpent. Because of the stubborn nature of Adam, who regarded Jehovah as the supreme God and creator of all existence, the fruit of the tree of knowledge could only first be conveyed to a woman. It was woman's non-acceptance and disobedience to the dictates of Jehovah that led her to eat of the enticing fruit of the Tree of Knowledge and share this with the man. This knowledge set the human race apart from all other created animals and made them unique to all creation. Due to his physical existence and his Satanically acquired knowledge and ability to reason, no creature is more beautiful than man—but most beautiful of all is woman.

Thus was the knowledge of the difference between light and darkness conveyed to man, and also the ability to choose between them. This is the knowledge that sets us free because it allows us the ability to understand the duality of the universe. Because of the spite of Jehovah, humankind was cursed and prevented from partaking of the fruit that would endow them of eternal physical existence. Therefore, the knowledge of Satan is also the knowledge of Death. We are unique beings because we possess the knowledge of the gods, yet we are cursed with a short physical life span. Thus with our freedom also comes responsibility. Physical existence is but a test in our natural ability to choose the correct path that will lead to the highest epitome of our collective destiny. As Satanists we recognize that it was Satan who set us free and it was Satan who shaped us to be what we are. We recognize that to fall into the Judeo/Christian/Muslim trap is to negate that which is our birthright as unique beings. It is our mission to learn what must be learned, do what must be done and convey that which must be conveyed. We must balance this with our freedom to take advantage of all the pleasures that physical existence has to offer because to not do so would negate the fact that we are both spiritual and physical beings.

And so to live as a Satanist is to perform a delicate balancing act that most of us will never fully understand until we are dead. Satan and the Demonic Spirits help us along the way as they will, but they also allow us to experience the effects of our mistakes that we might learn from them and become wise. We fall to our knees and worship only Satan in hopes that he will guide us to make the correct decisions, but also in tribute to the fact that we would not be as we are without the intervention of the Dark Divinity.

Chapter 2

The Satanic Gnosis

Gnosis basically means "knowledge" or "wisdom." The Gnosis in the Satanic context represents the knowledge conveyed by Satan in the form of the fruit of the Tree of Knowledge. Essentially, that knowledge is that the edicts of Jehovah which we have been led to believe are "good" are typically negative to our being and our development. The reverse is true about what is commonly considered "evil." Traditional Satanists look at the Christian Bible as an account of events that can be looked upon from two points of view. Such is the purpose of the Livri Luciferius; a text that reversed the values taught by the Christian Bible by illuminating phrases in the Bible which can be construed as Satanic. It also teaches us that Satan does not condemn us for such actions as lying, stealing and adultery because as free beings we must accept the consequences of our actions, positive or negative. Free existence is a double edged sword.

When seen from a Gnostic Satanic viewpoint, the Al-Jil-Wah imparts great wisdom because it sets down that Satan is the God and creator of the physical existence (as we know it) and puts forward a set of guidelines that we are to follow if we are to be successful in earthly Satanic endeavors (for instance we are told not to associate with non-Satanists because they cannot be trusted). Because man was able to acquire the Gnosis, we can also assume that Jehovah is not a supreme being and is obviously the creation of a very distant god. With this knowledge the duality of Light and Darkness can be viewed in a whole new context because it basically means that both Satan and Jehovah are divine beings. Knowing this, who would throw their lot in with Jehovah? If we are creations of Jehovah then we are (by proxy) also creations of the supreme and distant god. It is therefore logical to follow the dictates of Satan, who wishes us to rise to the highest level of our being. In light of such knowledge the Christian Bible can be viewed as an account of man's struggle against the false dictates of Jehovah. Our heroes of the Bible (and those accepted texts of the apocrypha) would be Lilith, Cain, Pharaoh Ramses II, the Endor Witch, Goliath, Enoch (son of Cain), Herodias and Judas Iscariot, to name a few. From a Satanic viewpoint these are the true Saints and martyrs of old. For example, John the Baptist is he who was sent by god to baptize the nations and therefore re-enslave them to Jehovah. The "holy" water is merely that which would cleanse us of the

Gnosis and revert man to a subservient state. It was Herodias who saw this doom and ordered the execution of John the Baptist, further adding that his head should be delivered to her on a platter. Such is the Will of humankind, to persevere above the entrapments of Jehovah and to take the necessary actions against those who are but agents of our annihilation! Possessing the Gnosis is the only way the individual Satanist can persevere against the traps that Jehovah sets for us. Knowledge is power, power is freedom. If we become victims to the Christian lie then we will surely lose all that was given to us.

Chapter 3

The Anti-Christ

The Anti-Christ is the one called the Beast in the Book of Revelations of the Christian Bible. He has yet to come and his number will be 666. To the Christians, he is an abomination because he will bring about the downfall of the Christian world. It is predicted in Revelations that he will unite most of the world under a single banner of Satan, and all the kingdoms loyal to him will know great joy. It is also predicted that the Nazarene will do battle with the Anti-Christ and that those allied to the Anti-Christ will fall. However, we must consider that the source of this prediction is a "God" that deceives man regarding the true nature of his ultimate power and influence. Hell exists untouched by Jehovah so where is their "God?" Satan was able to convey to man the Gnosis, and where was their "God?" Man is allowed to blaspheme even unto the gates of Heaven and where is their "God?" Truly Jehovah has lost most if not all his power and his servants are but blind idiots.

The Christians will turn the other cheek if confronted and so cannot possibly touch the hordes of Satan's legions clamoring at the Gates of Hell awaiting the Armageddon; after which all existence will be claimed in the name of Satan! And they shall behold his only begotten Son who is the Anti-Christ, a man totally endowed with the Spirit of Satan. Man alone has conquered the Nazarene in the past and made a mockery of his fragile body. He who weeps tears for Jesus should be cast out and utterly despised. On the day of the coming of the Anti-Christ, all Satanists, even those who are confused into believing that Satan is merely a symbol shall unite and receive the mark of the Beast.

The Christians have their era, and we are living in it right now. It is predicted that the coming age will proclaim the victory and glory of Satan, and in his kingdom the Evil and the Blasphemers shall no longer be crushed under the Christian heel. Let it be known that the Anti-Christ is the true savior of the Satanist, and all that is worthy in the world.

Chapter 4

Satan's Kingdom

The common misconception of Hell is that it is a burning lake of fire created by Jehovah for the Devil and his brood. This is not so! Satan is a creator and Hell is the spiritual kingdom created by him. It is a place that the hand of Jehovah has not touched. It is a place that Jehovah cannot peer into. It is a place where the souls of humans know not the sorrows of Christian torment. It is that place where we can truly be with our own kind. It is a mirror of the Universe itself, as conceived by Satan. And after Jehovah, the Nazarene, and all the souls of Christian swine have been placed into affliction by Satan, all creation shall become Hell.

The very matter of Hell is pure chaos reshaped into the darkest fantasies of the Satanic divinity. By its nature, Hell knows not the turmoil of physical existence, nor do its denizens know of the terror of expiration. It is that perfect place that lives in the heart and desires of every true Satanist. Those who are loyal and achieve their destiny in life shall join Satan's legions after death. The true will of the human is to fulfill his destiny, and Hell is the destiny of much of us. Those who deny it will only know regret that they deceived themselves in life. The destiny of every Satanist is to join Satan in Hell.

Chapter 5

Brother Myrmydon's 9 Laws of Demonic Spirit Contact

- Always use respectful conjurations when attempting to contact Demons.

- Always have the proper offerings/accouterments prepared for any Demon you attempt to contact.

- Never attempt to contact a Demon that you know nothing about.

- Always have a specific question/request for any Demon you attempt to contact.

- Do not attempt to "banish" a Demon at the end of your ritual.

- Do not form a "protective" circle when attempting to contact Demons.

- If you attempt to contact a Demon do not show any fear of whatever might manifest itself.

- Always name a specific Demon when attempting to make contact.

- Not all Demonic manifestations are immediately apparent.

Chapter 6

An Explanation of the 9 Laws

Always use respectful conjurations when attempting to contact Demons:

This one is the most obvious. We find in the LaVeyan texts that we should "command" the "forces" of Darkness to bestow infernal power upon us. It just isn't that simple. Considering that the LaVeyans do not believe in the entities that they call upon it is easy to see why they might do this. To them, Satanic Ritual is merely a gratification of the ego, but we, as Traditional Satanists, must know the Truth. Demons are very real and possess a conscience and power far beyond the abilities of mere humans. Do not believe the words of Bob Larson or what you might see in Exorcism horror movies. Demons cannot be brought down by the petitions of priests of any religion. If they appear to submit to a human being it is because they do so of their own free will. Any attempt to seriously command a Demon could have disastrous or even fatal consequences. Most would be lucky if they will not even manifest at all. Perhaps that is why Goetic Magicians believe them to be a thing of the human mind. Perhaps the only "Demons" they are "conjuring" are simply manifestations of their subconscious. The use of Christian prayers and threats will not raise a Demon unless they are angered.

Always have the proper offerings/accouterments prepared for any Demon you attempt to contact:

Anytime a Demon manifests on the physical plane it expends energy. If you truly wish to be successful, then you should be aware of the necessary accouterments for summoning each Demon. Usually the things a Demon prefers are those which replenish its expended energy.

Never attempt to contact a Demon that you know nothing about:

Not all Demonic spirits are friendly to humans. Caution should be especially taken when summoning those Demonic Spirits outside of the Traditional Pantheons.

Always have a specific question/request for any Demon you attempt to contact:

Demons do not like parlor tricks. If you are attempting to summon a Demon just to see if it exists then you are doing it for the wrong reasons.

Do not attempt to "banish" a Demon at the end of your ritual:

This is an old misconception only applicable in Wicca and Traditional Ceremonial Magick. It is necessary to banish "Demons" in these rituals because these systems are only calling upon thought forms. Seeing as how Demons we call upon are real entities, this would obviously be viewed as hostile and disrespectful.

Do not form a "protective" circle when attempting to contact Demons:

This is another obvious misconception of Traditional Magickal Systems. If you are of the Darkness, then you must not fear the Darkness. If you have reason to fear because you question the nature of the Demonic Spirit, or you do not know very much about it then you should not perform the ritual at all.

If you attempt to contact a Demon do not show any fear of whatever might manifest itself:

Summoning Demons can be very dangerous and should not be taken lightly. If you choose to do so then you must accept the consequences of your actions. What will be is what will be. All is destiny. We must accept the consequences of ANY actions we take, and we must not wallow in fear or regret. We must walk into every challenge with a whole heart.

Always name a specific Demon when attempting to make contact:

If you make a general petition to the forces of Darkness (as some others who are novice might suggest) you have no way of knowing what effect it might have, or if it will have any effect at all. We have no way of knowing if the specific Demon we petition will manifest itself, or if another will manifest instead. What we can be sure of is that if we are specific in our evocations then we can know that our results will be less varied in most instances.

Not all Demonic manifestations are immediately apparent:

Some individuals are born more receptive to the Spirit world than others. If you do the ritual and a Demon does not appear but your answer/solution becomes apparent at a later time, you can be sure that your ritual has been answered. Witnessing the visual manifestation of a Demonic Spirit is sometimes not a very pleasant experience, and in all cases a very nerve racking phenomenon. Perhaps it is better for your individual self that you do not see them. Many have good working relationships with Demons and never actually "see" or "experience" their full presence. Just because a Demon may not appear to have answered your petition does not mean that it does not exist. Just because a person does not believe in Demons does not void their existence. What "is" simply "is." Any human opinion regarding beliefs can only go as far as that individual's perception.

Chapter 7

DEMONS: *A Personal Testimony*

Demonic Spirits do exist! It is a fact of physical science (even though we are not advanced enough to prove it as such)! Like humans, Demons all have their own individual personalities and traits. Some are friendly to humans and some are hostile, even to Satanists. Interaction with Demons isn't a requirement of Traditional Satanism, although it is known that we can gain much by forming mutual relationships. The Traditional pantheon includes the 72 spirits that can be found in the Goetia. This is not all the Demons that exist; it is simply those which are most commonly known. Material regarding the Nine laws has already been presented in this book so I need not go into that any further. Rather I present a list of frequently asked questions and their answers.

Do Demons really possess people as in the movie "The Exorcist?"

Possession is known, but it is rare that a Traditional Satanist becomes possessed by Demons. However, this phenomenon is known all over the world, especially in certain sects of Voudou and Hinduism. "The Exorcist" is a work of fiction. In most cases, Demonic possession is not harmful to the host human.

Can Demons possess animals or statues?

Yes, I can personally attest to the fact that Demons possess animals, sometimes with startling results.

Can Demons manifest in such a way that I can see their physical form?

Yes, but do you really need to SEE a Demon to know that it exists?

Can Demons move objects and cause changes in the physical environment?

Yes! And this has been witnessed quite often.

Does every Satanist have a guardian Demon?

Every HUMAN has a guardian Demon. Much can be learned from the

Demon who holds power over the day you were born. It is known that the Demon who can convey the most is the Demon who holds power over the day you will die, but who really knows this for sure?

What are the 72 Demons, and where do they come from?

Some would say that they are the Fallen Angels who rebelled with Lucifer. Others would say that they are the spirits of the Nephilim. It is most commonly accepted that they are the half-breed spawn of Lilith and Cain, who were the first humans cast out of Jehovah's kingdom. No one really knows for sure.

How can I contact my Guardian Demon?

Every Satanist's relationship with the Demonic Spirits is separate and individual. It is first suggested that you undergo the self-initiation rite (as this is your formal introduction to the denizens of Hell and the proclamation of your allegiance) and then begin to slowly introduce yourself to your Guardian Demon. Above all follow your own instincts. Talk to the Demon as if it were a person standing in front of you. Confide in the Demon. It will manifest itself when the time is right, but always remember that your pact is with Satan/Lucifer and none can be held higher.

Chapter 8

The Names of the 36 Day Demons and the Dates Over Which They Preside

DAY DEMONS

1) BAAL March 21-30

2) AGARES March 31-April 10

3) VASSAGO April 11-20

4) SAMIGINA April 21-30

5) MARBAS May 1-10

6) VALEFOR May 11-20

7) AMON May 21-31

8) BARBATOS June 1-10

9) PAIMON June 11-20

10) BUER June 21-July 1

11) GUSION July 2-11

12) SITRI July 12-21

13) BELETH July 22-August 1

14) LERAJE August 2-11

15) ELIGOS August 12-22

16) ZEPAR August 23-September 1

17) BOTIS September 2-11

18) BATHIN September 12-22

19) SALLOS September 23- October 2

20) PURSON October 3-12

21) MARAX October 13-22

22) IPOS October 23- November 1

23) AINI November 2-12

24) NABERIUS November 13-22

25) GLASYALABOLAS November 23-December 2

26) BUNE December 3-12

27) RONOVE December 13-21

28) BERITH December 22-30

29) ASTAROTH December 31-January 9

30) FORNEUS January 10-19

31) FORAS January 20-29

32) ASMODEUS January 30-February 8

33) GAAP February 9-18

34) FURFUR February 19-28

35) MARCHOSIAS March 1-10

36) STOLAS March 11-20

Chapter 9

The Names of the 36 Night Demons and The Dates Over Which They Preside

NIGHT DEMONS

1) PHENEX March 21-30

2) HALPHAS March 31-April 10

3) MALPHAS April 11-20

4) RAUM April 21-30

5) FOCALOR May 1-10

6) VEPAR May 11-20

7) SABNACK May 21-31

8) SHAX June 1-10

9) VINE June 11-20

10) BIFRONS June 21-July 1

11) UVALL July 2-11

12) HAAGENTI July 12-21

13) CROCELL July 22-August 1

14) FURCAS August 2-11

15) BALAM August 12-22

16) ALLOCES August 23-September 1

17) CAMIO September 2-11

18) MURMUR September 12-22

19) OROBAS September 23-October 2

20) GREMORY October 3-12

21) OSE October 13-22

22) AMY October 23-November 1

23) ORIAX November 2-12

24) VAPULA November 13-22

25) ZAGAN November 23-December 2

26) VOLAC December 3-12

27) ANDRAS December 13-21

28) HAURES December 22-30

29) ANDREALPHUS December 31-January 9

30) CIMERES January 10-19

31) AMDUSIAS January 20-29

32) BELIAL January 30-February 8

33) DECARABIA February 9-18

34) SEERE February 19-28

35) DANTALION March 1-10

36) ANDROMALIUS March 11-20

BOOK II

Introduction

THE THREE-FOLD PURPOSE OF SELF INITIATION

This part of THE DEVIL'S BIBLE is included as an instructional guide for those solitary practitioners of Traditional Satanism . Initiation is very important, even to solitary Satanists. The self initiation rite in this book takes place over the course of 3 night, while the Coven initiation rite is done in one night. The intent of initiating one's self carries a three fold purpose...

TO COMPLETLEY SHED ANY PREVIOUS RELIGIOUS AFFILIATION OR PROGRAMMING:

This is symbolized by the practitioner wearing the white gown of innocence and purity. Whether you may have been a Christian, Jew, Moslem, atheist or Wiccan, all must be cast aside and surpassed on the first night of the ritual.

The practitioner will also wear the symbol of his previous religious affiliation. The Altar shall bear a white cloth and white candles will be lit. This is the ultimate blasphemy against the person we are before we become complete Satanists. The purpose of the ritual is to say a final goodbye to his/her former self and to obliterate utterly the part of him/herself that would choose any lord above Satan/Lucifer. The first ritual makes way for the second ritual in which the practitioner shall make his pact with Satan as a new person.

TO SELF-RECEIVE THE MARK OF THE BEAST, AND TO MAKE THE DEDICATION PACT WITH SATAN AS A NEW PERSON:

The white vestments and the symbol of previous religious ideology are discarded after the first night's ritual. The second ritual shall be done completely nude (this is symbolic of the fact that we are new to the world, as we are born). In this ritual the practitioner will offer a piece of his/her clothing (cut from the white gown) to Satan as a symbol of total loyalty. He shall give him/herself the mark of the beast to confirm his/her acceptance of the future coming of Satan's Kingdom and he/she shall submit the pact to Satan. The pact is defined as a contract given to Satan, stating ones intentions after they are accepted into the Devil's religion. It is highly personal, and every individual must decide for him/herself what they will promise to Satan.

TO MAKE ONES INTRODUCTION TO SATAN'S KINGDOM AS A NEW SATANIST WITH A NEW SATANIC NAME:

All vestments shall be in Black or Red. The Altar shall be set up per instructions found in this book and the practitioner shall now wear his/her Satanic ritual wear of choice. He/She shall introduce themselves to Satan's Kingdom and shall now forever identify with a new Satanic name. The third night's ritual completes the cycle.

Undertaking this ritual entails a lifetime commitment to Satan. You are making this choice of your own free will and giving your loyalty freely. There is no way to undo or make void the initiation ritual. Satanists do not half dedicate, or dedicate for a given period of time. A Brother or Sister of Hell is that for this life and for all time. If you choose to initiate yourself and you complete the ritual, you are forever tied to the pact you made with Satan. Acting against the promises you make to Hell holds most dire consequences. YOU WERE WARNED.

Chapter 1

First Night Ritual of Self-Initiation

Materials needed:

White gown

Black hilted ritual knife

Symbol of previous religious affiliation

White altar cloth

Two white candles

Shovel

THE RITUAL

NOTE: This ritual is an example written from the perspective of someone whose previous religious association is Christianity. If the practitioner's previous religious affiliation is something else, the ritual should be altered to fit the individual practitioner.

The white altar shall be set in place and the white candles shall be lit before the rite begins (if incense is to be employed it should be ambergris). The participant shall enter the ritual chamber wearing the white gown. He/She shall carry the Black Hilted Knife and a copy of ritual. The symbol of crucifix shall be worn.

PARTICIPANT: "In the name of my Lord Jesus Christ—NO! I shall no longer submit to the Nazarene nor shall I call him Lord. I come here this night to proclaim that Christianity is the religion of the weak! I have been weak and I have fallen into many delusions and errors for which I must recant. From this day forth I renounce Jesus Christ and Jehovah and I renounce any and all ties that I have had to the Christian Church. I see the Cross for what it represents...

(The crucifix is to be torn off and thrown on the altar)

...which is my DOOM! I shall no longer pay homage to Jesus...

(spit upon cross)

...I shall no longer pay homage to Jehovah...

(spit upon cross a second time)

...I shall no longer allow the Holy Spirit within me!

(spit upon cross a final and third time)

I formally renounce my Christian right to dwell with Jesus in heaven, for I recognize it were better that I cease to exist! So I pray thee, Lord Jesus, for the last time, erase me from the book of life and depart from me your eternal salvation!"

The white gown is to be torn off and a piece is to cut from it and set aside for a later purpose. The candles are now snuffed out. The gown, the candles, and the crucifix are all to be wrapped in the white altar cloth and taken to any outside location where they can be buried. With the shovel dig a hole at least two feet deep. Place the altar cloth in the hole and urinate or defecate upon it. Then cover the hole and retire to sleep without speaking to anyone.

THE FIRST RITUAL IS NOW COMPLETE

Chapter 2

Second Night Ritual of Self-Initiation

Materials needed:

one sterile needle

one India ink pen

two black candles

1 sheet of parchment or similar paper

the piece of white cloth cut from the gown

black bowl

THE RITUAL

The altar should be set up as sparse as possible. You will only need a surface of some sort to write upon, and the black candles should provide the only light. If incense is to be employed then it must be Jasmine or Cinnamon. The parchment should be set upon the altar, with the sterile needle and Indian ink pen handy. The Practitioner will be nude during the duration of the rite.

PARTICIPANT: "Having rejected Christ and my former self I now make my petition to join Satan's legions. I come here this night bearing with me a shred of my former robe that I might give this to Satan. The burning of this cloth is a symbol of the complete sacrifice of my Christian self, as it is a token of my obedience to the will of Satan."

(The Participant will now hold the cloth in the flame of the Black candle until it catches fire. He/She will then place the cloth into the bowl and wait until it is consumed and the fire goes out.)

"Having made my offering of submission I now take upon myself the mark of the beast. I am He (She) that hath wisdom, and I have calculated the number."

(Participant will now write upon his/her body '666' with the India ink. It matters not where the mark is placed)

"Having taken upon myself the mark of my new lord and savior, I am now ready to enter into a pact with my new Master. In nomine Ordo Novus Seclorum! In nomine Satanas!"

(The Participant will now write out his pact. What is written is entirely between the individual and Satan. Only understand that you will face dire consequences should you break your Oath. There is no such thing as temporary pact. If you belong to the Devil once, you belong to him forever. After the pact is written the practitioner should prick the webbed skin between his/her middle and ring finger on the left hand. When sufficient blood flow occurs, the practitioner shall sign the pact with his/her Christian name.)

"I give to Satan myself, body and soul effective now."

(Candles are snuffed out and the practitioner exists the ritual place.)

The Pact is never destroyed! It should be kept in a very special place to remind the practitioner of that Oath that he/she must abide by. People who incinerate their pacts often forget about the commitments they are sworn to.

THE SECOND RITUAL IS NOW OVER

Chapter 3

Third Night's Ritual of Self-Initiation

Materials Needed:

A full altar arrangement

A sword or dagger

A necklace bearing a satanic symbol (or ring of such)

A black bowl of water

THE RITUAL

The altar should be set up according to the Traditional Cathedral of the Black Goat format. The Practitioner will wear the black robe, or be clad all in black. The black bowl of water should be set upon the altar where it will be handy. If incense is to be employed it should be of sulfur or sandalwood.

PARTICIPANT: "I come here a changed man/woman. I have made my sacrifice; I have accepted the mark and the pact has been sealed. Demon's of the pit, I ask for your presence here! Shadows in the darkness, thou art welcome.

I come here now not as an outsider but as a humble servant."

(the participant will pick up the dagger/sword and proceed to call the corners as according to the standard public rite of The Cathedral of the Black Goat)

"May the wisdom of Lucifer fill me! May the Joy of Astaroth fill me! May the power of Beelzebub fill me! May the strength of Lilith fill me !"

(The participant will now point the dagger toward his/her own body and lightly trace the sign of the inverted pentagram. This will start with the left uppermost point on the left breast, then to the bottom point just above the genital area, then to the uppermost right point at the right breast, then down to the left middle point to the left of the navel, then across to the right of the navel and back up to the left breast)

"Sanctus Satanas! I have given up my former body and soul, and as a new child of Satan I must receive a dedicated name. I choose (new Satanic Name). And from this point forward I am this name to my Brothers and Sisters, and I will only stand before judgment under my Satanic name."

(Participant now dips his/her hands in the bowl of water and proceeds to anoint his/her head and face)

"Water of the river Acheron wash away the name of him/her who no longer is. Sanctus Satanas!"

(Participant now places the necklace or ring upon him/herself)

"With this token of Satan, whose symbol is born of fire I seal my connection to the denizens of Darkness. Sanctus Satanas!"

(The candles should now be snuffed out and the Participant should spend at least five minutes in prayer or contemplation, after which an exit is made)

THE THIRD RITUAL IS NOW OVER AND THE SELF-INITIATION IS COMPLETE

Chapter 4

The Satanic Altar

The Satanic Altar is one of the most important items in Traditional Satanism. The Altar acts as a central focal point for our worship, and a gateway to Satan's Kingdom. If you are to have an entire room dedicated to rituals, then the altar must be erected first. The ritual chamber is built around the altar.

The Altar should be as elaborate as you can make it. We as Satanists do not yet have the ability to attend a real Temple for our religious services, but for now we can at least do the best we can to create this atmosphere in the places where Christians cannot stop us. The beginning of the Altar should be a table of some sort covered by a black cloth and lined in red. It should be neat and clean and treated as if it were actually an artifact from Hell. There should be a cloth above the altar and it should have printed upon it the sigils of Satan/Lucifer, Astaroth, Lilith, and Beelzebub, as these are the four lords of Hell. An image of Satan (your choice) should be on display and act as a focal point of all rituals and devotions. Upon the Altar shall sit the black hilted knife or sword, chalice, offering plate (to hold the host), and the Black Book. The Black Book can contain many things such as the Al-Jilwah, Musef Resh, or the Livri Luciferius. It should also contain an account of the Public Ritual and any other things pertinent to the Coven or individual. Black Candles should be utilized however if this is not a possibility then the only alternative is red. The incense favored by the Cathedral Of The Black Goat are those that we have burned at the times of heightened supernatural ritual experiences. Who can say if the Demons prefer a particular kind of incense or even if they posses olfactory senses? In our experience the best incense is Ambergris, Jasmine, Cinnamon, Sandalwood, and Sulfur.

We realize that many must utilize portable altars because they fear someone living with them might find out about their Satanic affiliations. We understand this and we believe Satan understand this as well. In such a case we suggest that you have a portable altar small enough to fit under a bed or in a closet. When the portable altar is not in use it should be covered by a black cloth.

Chapter 5

Basic Devotional Prayers

Presented here are prayers to Lucifer and to Satan. The nature of the relationship between Satan and Lucifer is complicated because they are the light and dark aspects of the same being. As Satanists we tend to focus on the Satanic, though the Luciferian can be adapted for our use.

Suffice it to say that Satan is the greater aspect from October 31 to April 29. During this time the Satanic Prayer is to be said upon waking, and the Luciferian before sleep.

Lucifer is the greater aspect from April 30 to October 30. During this time the prayer to Lucifer is said upon waking.

The same holds true in our rituals. October 31 and April 30 are the Grey days in which Satan/Lucifer's influence is felt the most, and when the disciple will experience a 'sharpening', or peak in magickal power.

These prayers are not to serve as the extent of a practitioner's devotional practice, rather they are only the beginning. The problem with Today's Traditional Satanists is that they don't realize that they can talk to Satan and the demons at any time or place. Talk to Satan often! You may be surprised by the results.

PRAYER TO LUCIFER

Oh Mighty Lucifer,

Keep me in thy grace.

Light my path with the lamps of thy infernal light,

If it is thy will allow me to prosper that I may serve thee better.

Bring torment upon my enemies and those who would hinder my service to thee,

Let them forever burn in the fires of thy wrath.

Help me to experience and know the substance of thy being,

And keep me away from the deception of those who are without thy grace.

Know that my power is only what you allow,

For nothing is NOT.

Upon the demise of this body guide my soul to HELL,

For it is my wish to be with thee.

These things I ask--

Thy will be done on this black earth as it is in Hell.

For thine is light of my dominion, salvation and triumph--FOREVER

Ave Luciferi!

PRAYER TO SATAN

Oh Mighty Satan,

Save me from the treacherous and the violent.

Mark with vengeance those who would hinder me for I am your humble servant.

Thou art the Lord of the darkest pit that brings my soul to greatest Joy.

Thou art the one and original innovator of humanity, those who can not see this deserver no pity.

I ask that you place in my path those who will be destroyed by me, grant me the power to do so.

I ask that you place in my path those puzzles that I am to solve, grant me the wisdom to do so.

I ask that you place in my path those challenges that I am to overcome, grant me the strength to do so.

Be my path left or right, my final destination is your kingdom.

That which is to die, will die.

That which is to burn, shall burn.

He/She who is to find salvation in the arms of the Dark Lord shall do so.

For the Lord of my destiny is Satan!

Ave Satanas!

Chapter 6

The Public Mass of the Cathedral Of The Black Goat

This is the basic structure of the group ritual performed by the Cathedral Of The Black Goat. It can be added on to or altered depending upon the occasion and needs of the participants. This ritual can also substitute the Grey mass practiced on December 29 so long as the altar cloth and ritual candles are grey. Notice that the name of 'Lucifer' is called upon in the example given. If this ritual was being conducted between October 31- April 29, it would be Satan called upon instead.

The ritual must have at least 4 participants to be performed correctly. There must be a Priest(ess), a celebrant, a deacon and at least 1 person minimum to serve as the congregation.

Vestments

ALTAR-The altar cloth should be Black and Red (to represent Satan) or Blue and White (To represent Lucifer). The candles should be black or brown and they should sit in holders on the right and the left side of the idol. An Idol is defined as any statue, picture, or other rendering that depicts Satan or a particular demonic spirit. There shall be a chalice of either wine, water or apple juice. There shall be a black plate upon which the hosts shall sit. A host in this context is defined as any wheat product (bread or crackers and such) that shall server as the body of Satan.

Some covens feel it is wrong to consume the body of Satan and so they substitute apple slices (to represent the fruit from the tree of knowledge) instead. Either way is acceptable.

PRIEST(ess): Shall be robed in plain black with a red girdle. He (she) shall have the book of the coven in which this ritual is to be hand written. A triangular hood with two eye slits is traditional, however this is optional.

CELEBRANT: The celebrant wears a red robe or cloak and a black girdle is optional. The celebrant is armed with the weapon of the working. The weapon of the working is defined as any sword or dagger used to call the corners at the beginning of the ceremony. There shall be a pentagram inscribed on the floor (or a rug for those of you who have carpeted ritual rooms) and the celebrant shall not leave the circle for the duration of the ritual.

DEACON: The deacon shall wear a black cloak or robe with a purple girdle optional. It is the deacon's duty to lead the congregation into the ritual room, light the candles, and pass out the wine and host at the proper time. If anything goes wrong during the ritual (such as someone knocking on the front door, a dog barking, etc) it is the deacon's job to handle it.

CONGREGATION: Shall be dressed all in black with shoes removed . It is a good idea to provide missals (booklets) containing the parts that the congregants shall say during the ritual.

The ritual begins when all is set in place. The candles are lit and the deacon goes out to retrieve the congregation from an adjacent waiting area. The Priest and Celebrant should already be in place. The Celebrant inside the Pentagram and the Priest standing in the east (the altar should face south).

Priest: I proclaim this the sabbat night of the Cathedral of the Black Goat . Let this dwelling place be sanctified in the name of our masters.....

LUCIFER!

(Celebrant points sword east)

ASTAROTH!

(Celebrant points sword south)

BEELZEBUB!

(Celebrant points sword west)

LILITH!

(Celebrant points sword north)

CELEBRANT: By the conquering worm that hath swallowed the sun, be there power mighty amongst us!

PRIEST: Lord Satan who art the shadow of the Christian god whose presence cannot withstand thee, I speak these words of agony for thy glory. Thou art doubt and revolt, pride and knowledge. Thou livest again in us and around us though it be a troubled time when our enemy doth reign. Today thy sons and daughters are scattered and celebrate thy cults in their hideouts. But thy people have increased! We know that our Dark Lord looks upon us with pride that thy true and orthodox ones are united. This world that denies thee thou inhabits, and the creator can only be blind with envy. Thou hast won Oh Satan—though anonymous and obscure for a few years yet. But the coming age shall proclaim thy revenge!

Thou shalt be reborn again in the Anti-Christ!

The science of mysteries, spurting suddenly like a black wave already quenches the thirst of the curious and uneasy. Men and Women see themselves mirrored in these waves of illusion which intoxicate and madden. Oh beautiful Satan, Black Goat of the World, I have fallen in love with thy tearstained face. The treacherous hordes of Christians shall tremble before thy mighty hand!

CONGREGATION: AVE SATANAS!

PRIEST: Oh mighty Lord Satan, liberator of all, we implore thy presence amongst us, HEAR OUR CALL! We come here in an attitude of worship, that thou might grace us with thy Lordship.

DEACON: Lord of Darkness, Lord of Fire, in our hearts all others are forgotten for it is thee that we desire.

PRIEST: And if under a Black Moon know that thy witches and thy warlocks will faithfully dance unto thee. They shall feast unto thee and they shall drink unto thee! As it was, so now it be!

ALL FEMALE PARTICIPANTS: GLORY TO THE HORNS THAT IMPALE THE INFIDEL AND THE ROTTEN!

ALL MALE PARTICIPANTS: GLORY TO THE MILK OF THY BREAST, BLESSINGS TO SHOW US WE ARE NOT FORGOTTEN!

ALL FEMALE PARTICIPANTS: GLORY TO THY PHALLIC ROD!

ALL MALE PARTICIPANTS: GLORY TO THY HOOVES THAT SHALL TRAMPLE THE CHRISTIAN GOD!

ALL PARTICIPANTS: GLORY AND WORSHIP BE TO THEE, AS SATAN WILLS SO SHALL IT BE!

PRIEST: And so it is that Satan's progeny be scattered.

However the sons and daughters of Lilith, ye the very bloodline of Cain shall reunite. Though it is that we are alike in blood to the infidel, spiritually we are a different people. Ye it is the right and responsibility of those who are chosen to rekindle the black flame and partake of thy essence ('partake of thy gift' if apple is being substituted for the host). When human and Satan become one a power ensues that cannot be undone!

(DEACON now lifts plate containing the host. CELEBRANT gives the plate a single tap with the sword saying the following incantation)

DEACON: By the power of this whack, be this bread thy essence black.

(The DEACON then distributes the host to all the CONGREGATION; serving then the PRIEST, CELEBRANT, and him/herself last).

(DEACON now lifts Chalice containing wine. CELEBRANT gives plate a single tap with the following incantation).

By the power of this thud be this wine our Master's blood!

And so thy Black Witches tread upon the earth with thy power in we that thy will can be.

-At this time the ritual should receive a proper closing, the candles should be extinguished, and the congregation should be led to a waiting area outside the ritual chamber.

BOOK III

THE BLACK BOOK OF SATAN THE AL JILWAH

CHAPTER I

..I WAS, AM NOW, AND SHALL HAVE NO END. I EXERCISE DOMINION OVER ALL CREATURES AND OVER THE AFFAIRS OF ALL WHO ARE UNDER THE PROTECTION OF MY IMAGE. I AM EVER PRESENT TO HELP ALL WHO TRUST IN ME AND CALL UPON ME IN TIME OF NEED. THERE IS NO PLACE IN THE UNIVERSE THAT KNOWS NOT MY PRESENCE. I PARTICIPATE IN ALL THE AFFAIRS WHICH THOSE WHO ARE WITHOUT CALL EVIL BECAUSE THEIR NATURE IS NOT SUCH AS THEY APPROVE. EVERY AGE HAS ITS OWN MANAGER, WHO DIRECTS AFFAIRS ACCORDING TO MY DECREES. THIS OFFICE IS CHANGEABLE FROM GENERATION TO GENERATION, THAT THE RULER OF THIS WORLD AND HIS CHIEFS MAY DISCHARGE THE DUTIES OF THEIR RESPECTIVE OFFICES EVERYONE IN HIS OWN TURN. I ALLOW EVERYONE TO FOLLOW THE DICTATES OF HIS OWN NATURE, BUT HE THAT OPPOSES ME WILL REGRET IT SORELY.

NO GOD HAS A RIGHT TO INTERFERE IN MY AFFAIRS, AND I HAVE MADE IT AN IMPERATIVE RULE THAT EVERYONE SHALL REFRAIN FROM WORSHIPPING ALL GODS. ALL OF THE BOOKS OF THOSE WHO ARE WITHOUT ARE ALTERED BY THEM;

AND THEY HAVE DECLINED FROM THEM, ALTHOUGH THEY WERE WRITTEN BY THE PROPHETS AND THE APOSTLES. THAT THERE ARE INTERPOLATIONS IS SEEN IN THE FACT THAT EACH SECT ENDEAVORS TO PROVE THAT THE OTHERS ARE WRONG AND TO DESTROY THEIR BOOKS.

TO ME TRUTH AND FALSEHOOD ARE KNOWN. WHEN TEMPTATION COMES, I GIVE MY COVENANT TO HIM THAT TRUSTS IN ME. MOREOVER, I GIVE COUNCIL TO THE SKILLED DIRECTORS, FOR I HAVE APPOINTED THEM FOR PERIODS THAT ARE KNOWN TO ME. I REMEMBER NECESSARY AFFAIRS AND EXECUTE THEM IN DUE TIME. I TEACH AND GUIDE THOSE WHO FOLLOW MY INSTRUCTION. IF ANYONE OBEY ME AND CONFORM TO MY COMMANDMENTS, HE SHALL HAVE JOY, DELIGHT AND COMFORT.

CHAPTER II

I REQUITE THE DECENDANTS OF ADAM, AND REWARD THEM WITH VARIOUS REWARDS THAT I ALONE KNOW. MOREOVER, POWER AND DOMINION OVER ALL THAT IS ON EARTH, BOTH THAT WHICH IS ABOVE AND THAT WHICH IS BENEATH, ARE IN MY HANDS. I DO NOT ALLOW FRIENDLY ASSOCIATON WITH OTHER PEOPLE, NOR DO I DEPRIVE THEM THAT ARE MY OWN AND THAT OBEY ME OF ANYTHING THAT IS GOOD FOR THEM. I PLACE MY AFFAIRS IN THE HANDS OF THOSE WHOM I HAVE TRIED AND WHO ARE IN ACCORD WITH MY DESIRES. I APPEAR IN DIVERSE MANNERS TO THOSE WHO ARE FAITHFUL AND UNDER MY COMMAND.

I GIVE AND TAKE AWAY; I ENRICH AND IMPOVERISH; I CAUSE BOTH HAPPINESS AND MISERY. I DO ALL THIS IN KEEPING WITH THE CHARACTERISTICS OF EACH EPOCH. AND NONE HAS A RIGHT TO INTERFERE WITH MY MANAGEMENT OF AFFAIRS. THOSE WHO OPPOSE ME I AFFLICT WITH DISEASE; BUT MY OWN SHALL NOT DIE LIKE THE SONS OF

ADAM THAT ARE WITHOUT. NONE SHALL LIVE IN THIS WORLD LONGER THAN THE TIME SET BY ME; AND IF I SO DESIRE, I SEND A PERSON A SECOND OR THIRD TIME INTO THIS WORLD OR INTO SOME OTHER BY THE TRANSMIGRATION OF SOULS.

CHAPTER III

I LEAD TO THE STRAIGHT PATH WITHOUT A REVEALED BOOK; I DIRECT ARIGHT MY BELOVED AND CHOSEN ONES BY UNSEEN MEANS. ALL MY TEACHINGS ARE EASILY APPLICABLE TO ALL TIMES AND ALL CONDITIONS. I PUNISH IN ANOTHER WORLD ALL WHO DO CONTRARY TO MY WILL.

NOW THE SONS OF ADAM DO NOT KNOW THE STATE OF THINGS THAT IS TO COME. FOR THIS REASON THEY FALL INTO MANY ERRORS. THE BEASTS OF THE EARTH, THE BIRDS OF HEAVEN AND THE FISH OF THE SEA ARE ALL UNDER THE CONTROL OF MY HANDS. ALL TREASURES AND HIDDEN THINGS ARE KNOWN TO ME; AND AS I DESIRE, I TAKE THEM FROM ONE AND BESTOW THEM UPON ANOTHER.

I REVEAL MY WONDERS TO THOSE WHO SEEK THEM, AND IN DUE TIME MY MIRACLES TO THOSE WHO RECEIVE THEM FROM ME. BUT THOSE WHO ARE WITHOUT ARE MY ADVERSARIES, HENCE THEY OPPOSE ME. NOR DO THEY KNOW THAT SUCH A COURSE IS AGAINST THEIR OWN INTERESTS, FOR MIGHT, WEALTH AND RICHES ARE IN MY HANDS, AND I BESTOW THEM UPON EVERY WORTHY DECENDANT OF ADAM. THUS THE GOVERNMENT OF THE WORLDS, THE TRANSITION OF GENERATIONS, AND THE CHANGES OF THEIR DIRECTORS ARE DETERMINED BY ME FROM THE BEGINNING.

CHAPTER IV

I WILL NOT GIVE MY RIGHTS TO OTHER GODS. I HAVE ALLOWED THE CREATION OF FOUR SUBSTANCES, FOUR TIMES AND FOUR CORNERS; BECAUSE THEY ARE NECESSARY THINGS FOR CREATURES.

THE BOOKS OF JEWS, CHRISTIANS AND MUSLIMS, AS OF THOSE WHO ARE WITHOUT, ACCEPT IN A SENSE, I.E., SO FAR AS THEY AGREE WITH AND CONFORM TO MY STATUTES. WHATSOEVER IS CONTRARY TO THESE, THEY HAVE ALTERED; DO NOT ACCEPT IT. THREE THINGS ARE AGAINST ME AND I HATE THREE THINGS. BUT THOSE WHO KEEP MY SECRETS SHALL RECEIVE THE FULFILLMENT OF MY PROMISES. THOSE WHO SUFFER FOR MY SAKE I WILL SURELY REWARD IN ONE OF THE WORLDS.

IT IS MY DESIRE THAT ALL MY FOLLOWERS UNITE IN A BOND OF UNITY, LEST THOSE WHO ARE WITHOUT PREVAIL AGAINST THEM. NOW, THEN, ALL YE WHO HAVE FOLLOWED MY COMMANDMENTS AND MY TEACHINGS, REJECT ALL THE TEACHINGS AND SAYINGS OF SUCH AS ARE WITHOUT. I HAVE NOT TAUGHT THESE TEACHINGS, NOR DO THEY PROCEED FROM ME. DO NOT MENTION MY NAME NOR MY ATTRIBUTES, LEST YE REGRET IT; FOR YE DO NOT KNOW WHAT THOSE WHO ARE WITHOUT MAY DO.

CHAPTER V

O YEA THAT HAVE BELIEVED IN ME, HONOR MY SYMBOL AND MY IMAGE, FOR THEY REMIND YOU OF ME. OBSERVE MY LAWS AND STATUTES. OBEY MY SERVANTS AND LISTEN TO WHATEVER THEY MAY DICTATE TO YOU OF THE HIDDEN THINGS. RECEIVE THAT, THAT IS DICTATED, AND DO NOT CARRY IT BEFORE THOSE WHO ARE WITHOUT, JEWS, CHRISTIANS, MUSLIMS AND OTHERS; FOR THEY

KNOW NOT THE NATURE OF MY TEACHING. DO NOT GIVE THEM YOUR BOOKS, LEST THY ALTER THEM WITHOUT YOUR KNOWLEDGE. LEARN BY HEART THE GREATER PART OF THEM, LEST THEY BE ALTERED...

BOOK IV

Addendum

The New Satanic Orthodoxy

When the Devil's Bible was first written, worshiping the Devil was still a bit of a taboo within the above ground Satanist scene. Indeed most had adopted the Church of Satan stance of getting nearly hysterical at the mere suggestion that they worshiped Satan or even believed in Satan. Very well then. Cathedral of the Black Goat was not created in the first place to "fit in" with their definition of Satanism or their so-called "Satanic community." In fact there is nothing more I despise than misfits who couldn't fit in with the Church of Satan, so they start their own groups using LaVey's book as a basis and are essentially LaVeyan Satanists but not Church of Satan. At the very least, they are just copy cats, uncreative no motivation—essentially intellectual leeches. But mainly, they are not reforming anything, not correcting the flaws of LaVeyan Satanism by essentially re-creating his wheel. In my opinion the fatal flaw of LaVeyanism is that it is called Satanism at all. LaVey himself had addressed this issue when he was alive. He stated that people would often exclaim to him, "Mr. Lavey, you have a great philosophy, but why call it Satanism at all, why not just call it humanism?" To which LaVey's reply was "because it is the most stimulating under that definition." So there you have it. Even he admits it is not Satanism, but in order to motivate his followers he will still call it that. That makes everything he ever wrote about his so called Satanism COMPLETLEY unacceptable to one who endeavors to worship the Devil. Regressing back to the showman carney attitude of false Satanism can only ever be a stumbling block to attaining true Light of Lucifer. Hence that was my starting point for creating the Cathedral of the Black Goat. Others such as Terry Taylor had done it before me, but they didn't leave much behind for us to go off of, hence Cathedral of the Black Goat is the first fully functional above ground Devil Worship Church of the 21st century, and this book is it's Manifesto—The Mein Kampf of a Devil Worshiper surrounded by decadent LaVeyan Satanism and presenting a Final solution. A return to Satanic Orthodoxy—Devil Worship of the middle ages and the Elizabethan era reborn in the age of tv, computers, the internet and mass media. The First edition of this book had done very well for an independently published work. As the Cathedral of the Black Goat became even more well known and established I noticed a peculiar phenomenon. What had happened to LaVey was happening to the Cathedral of the Black Goat. Bastard children organizations began popping up everywhere—Joy of Satan, theistic Satanism movement, Brotherhood of Satan, mostly involving ex-members of the Cathedral of the Black Goat. One group wants to drop the entire Satanic theology and make it some sort of alien or UFO garbage. Another tries to incorporate wiccan ideas and a liberal "more correct, socially acceptable" philosophical basis, while the other wants to make friends with LaVeyan Satanists and say that we are some kind of Brotherhood. Treason! Not to me because I never gave much attention to my detractors, but to Lord Satan and his would be followers who get caught up with these misfits and their stumbling blocks. That point cannot be overstated, yet it is essentially not important enough to overshadow our work here. If anything they show us exactly what we can degenerate into if we let our guard down and compromise even for a moment. Compromise is the greatest enemy to keeping this movement alive, because if we allow for that over the decades the original intent will be lost. Our integrity is worth so much more than making friends. If anything associating with misfits and their so called groups will make genuine potential Devil Worshipers think twice before associating with us. Therefore it became necessary to release The Devil's Bible in a third edition, that any Orthodox/Traditional Satanists can build upon themselves and build upon their relationship with the Master, Our Lord Satan.

The Exclusion Of Those Who Are Without

The present state of Traditional/Orthodox Satanism (Though the public may be aware of the existence of the Cathedral of the Black Goat) is primarily that of an underground cult. As explained in the Al-Jilwah, when the truth is known by one of the Sons of Adam, it shall be known to all. This is most likely an allusion to the time when Satan claims victory over the enemy, and all the cosmos and all creation are his. However, until that time the practice of our religion belongs to the few and the elite. Those who are without simply aren't good enough. Christianity, Islam and Judaism are very commercially cheap religions demanding very little from their follows save that they obey blindly and finance their temples of deceit and abstinence. They should remain separate from us due to their lack of vision and their overall lack of desire to become more than mindless drones. It isn't our job to evangelize to them, nor would we want to share our rituals with such undeserving peons of the universe. The sheep cry out, but we have no pity for their lot in life. The same must go for other individuals who demonstrate a lack of vision. What is wicca? Practicing the worship and superstitions of ancient peoples so weak that they were conquered by the sheep thousands of years ago. If their pantheon of nature gods and goddesses was so strong then how is it they have been muted from existence? Indeed the Wiccan pretends to be liberated and above Christianity, yet they are too afraid to take upon themselves the mark of the adversary. Further evidence of their weakness can be seen in the philosophy of their three fold law by which no individual can rise above another without equal retribution from their pitiful nature gods. Even more puzzling is the cowardice displayed by LaVeyans and others who by the virtue of paradox claim to be both Atheist and Satanist. They claim that the reason they do not worship Satan is because they have never seen him, so why do they imitate the rituals and image of the Traditional Devil Worshiper? Indeed ours is a noble image, but such dark rites demand a discipline and a price that they either cannot fathom, or as I suggested above are AFRAID to explore. Not worth our time. Not worthy to call themselves our Brothers and Sisters. Until the age where Satan reigns and his truth is known by all, Satan's Cult shall remain only for the exclusive, and those who are without will be excluded. They can only hunger for what they cannot have, and thirst for experiences they will never know.

What Exactly Do You Stand For?

It could be said that all politics and philosophical endeavors are worthless without a firm ground to stand upon. Most political systems and methods of philosophy all end at the same point unless one has a unique way of looking at them and pursuing them. Through the eyes of one who worships the Devil is one such unique view. Think about this for a moment, what exactly it is that you put your faith in......

Do you really believe that the non-Satanist popular politician can save you from all your ills by his or her hands alone? Can a secular philosopher thoroughly grounded in the cause of humanism give you the best advice on how to live your life as a Satanist? If we are to serve Satan and live this life in the way he intended, then Satan must be the starting and ending point of everything we do. As humans we may have great pride in the endeavors and advancements of whatever culture or society we belong to, or may have great expectations for our children, spouse, friends and family that surround us. Does this mean that if our society, children, spouse, friends or family disappoint us or betray us that it is the end of our world? How could that ever be if we put our ultimate faith in Satan and make him the beginning and ending of everything we do and the way we live? Ultimately if we place every ounce of spiritual, physical and emotional energy in the deeds of other humans we are setting ourselves up for failure, disappointment and ultimately depression. It is the plight of the world that we ate of the tree and partook of Satan's essence without fully realizing the potential of his presence within our individual lives. Turning to Satan will not save you from all the ills of this confused human society, however he will give you a strong foundation to build upon so that when your towers of expectation crumble in the face of this world, you will still have that foundation to build upon. The Arm of our master stretches from the east to the west and his promise can be yours if you but take his hand.

Destiny And The Nobility Of Evil

In every story their must be an antagonist. Whether this Antagonist wins out in the end depends upon the author. It is a cosmic law that the greatest of lights is only as strong as the darkness that foreshadows them. Without an antagonist we can only be faced with an obliteration of all thought, an eternity that leads to no where, the ultimate goal of Christianity. What is eternal life worth if death never existed? What are the so called Joys of Heaven without comparison to the so called fires of Hell? What is the worth of Choosing Good if a being never had the choice to begin with? Such is the holy duality of the universe manifested in the twin horns of the Black Goat. Antagonism itself is a holy law of the universe, the struggle that first brought life into existence. Our existence as Satan worshipers are a noble and sacred duty of the universe, something that no Christian with his destructive ideas of "oneness" can ever take away. When we are one, we will be one with Satan. We are the villains of this story, and some of us may find ourselves the villains in our own individual lives. This is something we should find solace in, it is our calling. There are so many souls across this world wandering the plains of life and death that do not know who they really are or what the universe has in store for their destiny. Hypocrisy is a crime generally committed by those who outwardly express strong opinions that are contrary to their true natures and ultimate Will. The ultimate peace does not come by deciding which master to serve, but by doing and living what it is that you are ultimately meant to do and be. If you find yourself walking the path of the Devil, and you can feel in your soul that it is what you were destined to do, then no Joys or Fires or religions of fear can deter you from peace and ultimate wholeness.

The Eternal Crede Of The Masters Of Darkness

The ultimate goal of worshiping Satan is to form a relationship with Satan and his demons

In so doing we transcend human emotions such as love, hate and fear and think in terms of what is realistically possible and impossible.

Life is but an endless barrage of possibilities in which we must evaluate and initiate the will of Satan with every given action.

We use prayer and ritual as a means of communicating openly with Satan. It is 'How' we determine what he asks of us, and where we discover the means by 'How' we will serve him.

There is no 'why' because 'why' was determined by Satan in the beginning.

For every challenge that Satan brings before us we learn what we are capable and incapable of overcoming.

We will always think in terms of the possible and impossible when contemplating how to carry out Satan's Will and not in terms of love, hate or fear.

If we find a task to be impossible, we will re evaluate our plan of action and cross reference it to the possible risk or cost resulting from the outcome.

The Ultimate Will of Satan (achieving it) outweighs the risk or cost of the individual charged with carrying out his will.

The Will of Satan does not serve those who are not his children.

All the powers of darkness are at our disposal if it is the will of Satan.

We shall carry out the will of Satan with anger and aggression as necessary in the pursuit of our desire to acheive his will.

While we occupy this human vessel we are fraught with many desires which accompany this sphere. While they shall not be ignored, our unearthly desire to sow the will of Satan is paramount.

We shall deliberately engage in exercises that strengthen our body, mind and will.

The strong always triumph over the weak as darkness shall always triumph over light.

The arts of mystery and occult shall be applied when necessary, but are ultimately insignificant next to the power of Satan.

If a man attacks you with a knife, bludgeon him with a hammer.

Be mindful of your surroundings, and never get caught off guard.

View every inconsistency in your life as only a temporary setback that you will overcome in the grand scheme of achieving the will of Satan.

One Satanic prayer is worth a thousand crucified Christs.

Before Satan Fell he was Lucifer. When Satan conquers our enemy he will again be Lucifer. Lucifer is the name of the God becoming.

When we give mercy to our enemy, we kill a part of ourselves.

There is nothing more beautiful than the purity of Evil.

Hail Satan, Betrayer of the Betrayer!

The reality we know is only a prelude to Satan's Kingdom.

By submitting to Satan totally, we make of ourselves vessels of his power and will.

SEVERED HEAD PUBLISHING

severedheadpublishing@yahoo.com

www.lulu.com/severedhead

www.severedheadpublishing.synthasite.com

www.myspace.com/severedheadpublishing

Severed Head Publishing Logo by Justin Jackley

www.justinjackley.com

Cover Design by Jim Ormston

www.myspace.com/demiurgegraphix

james_ormston@hotmail.com

Lightning Source UK Ltd.
Milton Keynes UK
178627UK00002B/92/P